HISTORICAL MEERKATS

CAESAR

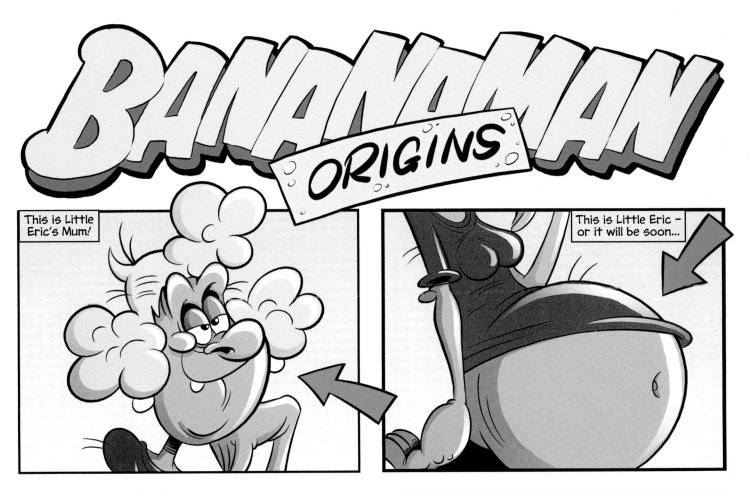

At first, baby Eric was a perfectly normal baby – belching, farting and dribbling at both ends, but strange events were about to unfold...

CORPORAL CLOTT

Corporal Cott is on the firing range...

Good grief!

POW POP PING

PING POP POW

Corporal Clott! That has to be the worst shooting I have ever seen!!!

Get me that target!

Sir! Yes, sir!

I can't believe it! How did you manage to hit the target so often?

It's easier if you put all the holes in the target before you put it all the way back there!

WHAT!?!

Oops! Did I say that out loud?

As a punishment, Colonel Grumbly sends Corporal Clott on a ten mile hike...

Mutter, grumble, stupid boy...

Huff

Puff

...mutter, makes my life a, mutter... grumble...

Wish I'd never set eyes on... mutter...

Causes more trouble than the bloomin' enemy!

Wha! Hoo!

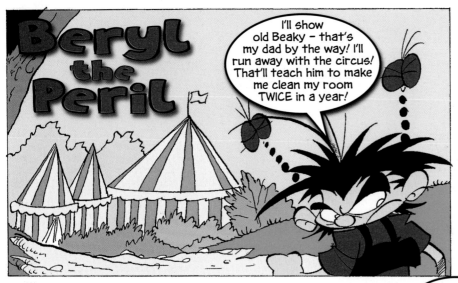

Beryl the Peril

I'll show old Beaky – that's my dad by the way! I'll run away with the circus! That'll teach him to make me clean my room TWICE in a year!

That'll be the door for me thataway!

Run aways Entrance

Trades mans Entrance

Hey! Who runs this joint?

The guy in the top hat – now let go of my wire!

SHRIEK!

Hoi, top hat guy – we need to talk!

TWANG

No, I think you'll find that we don't need to talk!

Yes, we do, mate! I'm Beryl the Periloni and I'm your new star attraction!

Oh, yes? And what exactly can you do? Can you tame lions?

Can I? Can I tame lions? Watch this!

No! She didn't just do what I thought she did, did she?

THWAX

Y-You knocked him out!

You asked if I could tame lions – well, this one looks pretty tame to me!

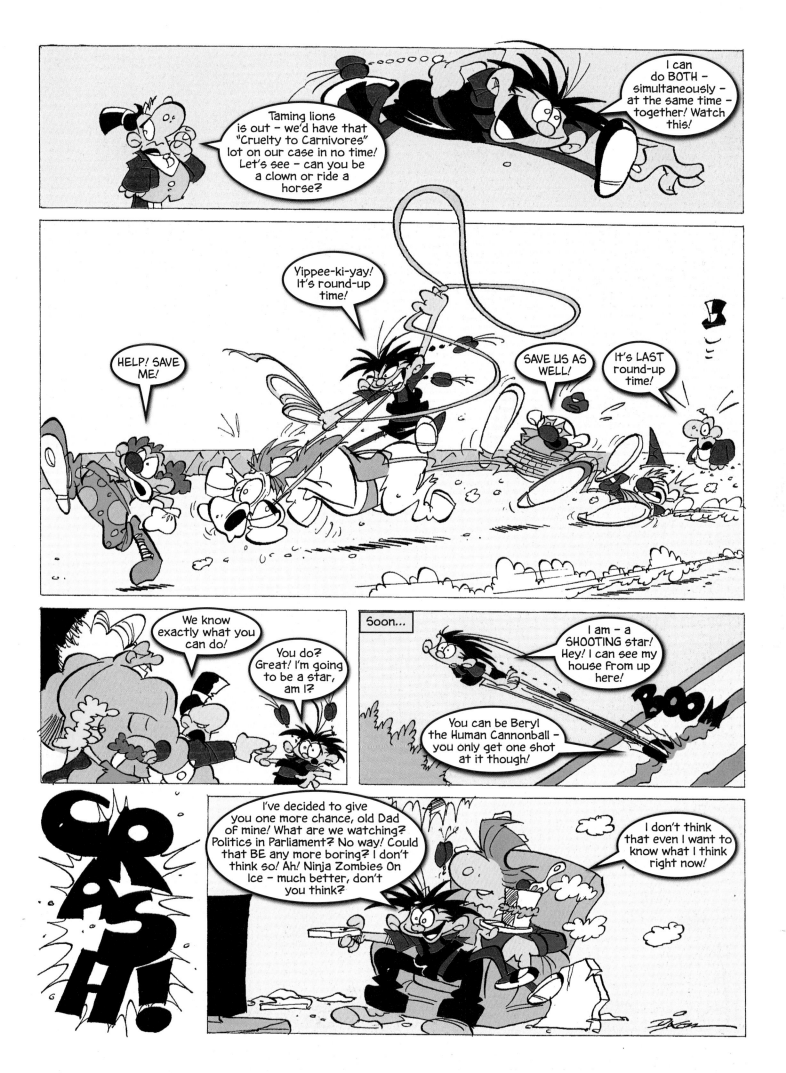

George vs Dragon

CLEOPATRA

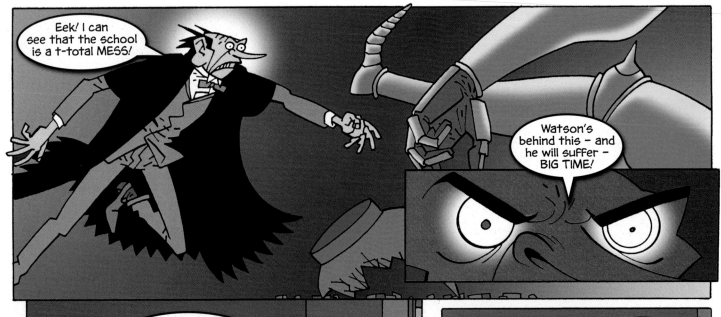

This isn't the Dark Ages, Creep! Pupils must be treated with kindness and respect!

To make it up to them, we're sending them on a week's break to Disneyland...

...and YOU'LL be paying for it – out of your wages!

Whine!

Reee-sult!

So...

This is wicked, Winker – but what happened to Gizmo?

Well, I thought Creepy would be lonely all by himself...

...so I left Gizmo at Greytowers as a playmate for him!

Erk! Eek! Do y-you know, there ARE t-times when I don't really like Watson!

STREF'

WILLIAM THE CONKEROR MEERKAT

Puss and Boots

Aw, cool! It's Puss and Boots! These guys are great! They're always knocking the stuffing out of each other...

Lets just watch...

Any second now, it's all going to kick off...

Aw, come on!!!

CLANG!

Oh dear, what happened to you?

Ouh?

Someone hit me with a frying pan!

You!

You have a frying pan behind your back!!!

That's just a coincidence. It could have been anyone.

GRRR! How come I've just logged onto your Twitter account, and it says "Just hit Puss with a frying pan! LOL!"

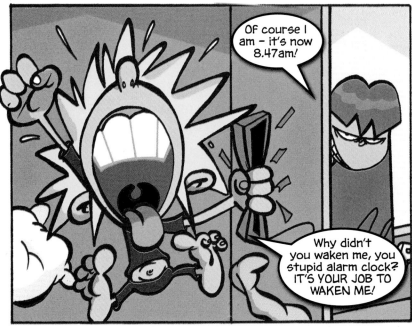

BULLY BEEF and CHIPS

CORPORAL CLOTT

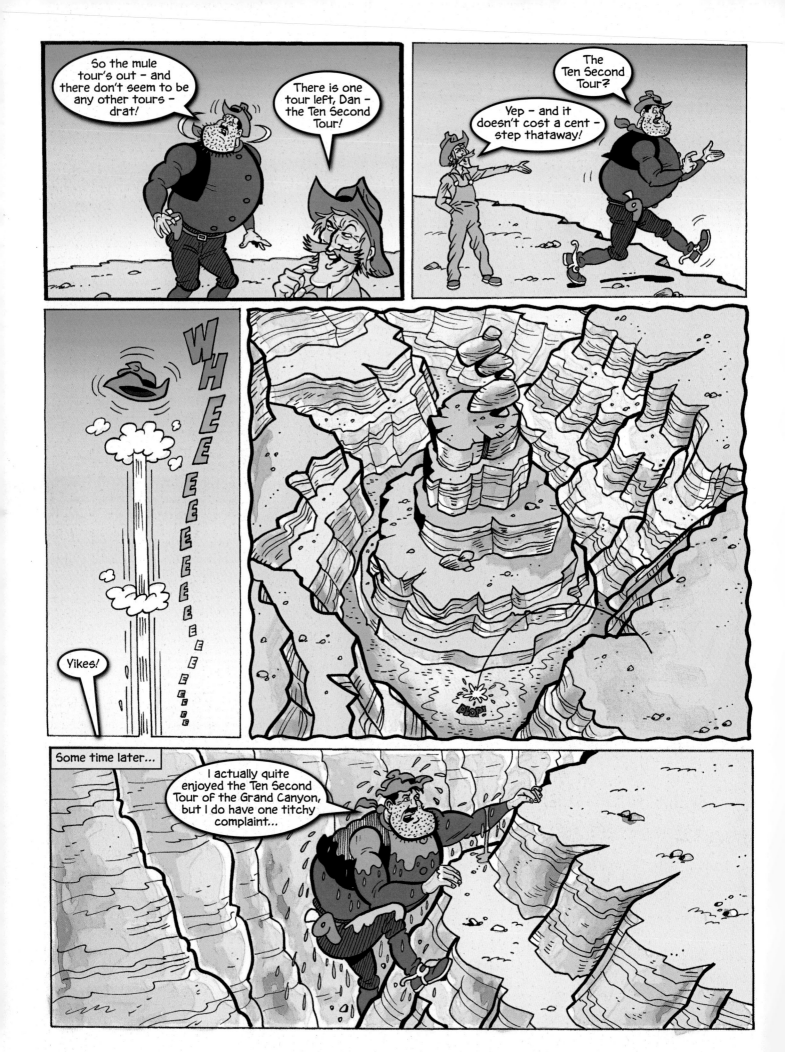

KID COPS

Ollie Fliptrik

Woo-hoo! What a buzz!

Watch it, Ollie – you're grabbing too much air!

KRAK

Told you!

Oh, man! I've broken another deck!

That's the third this month!

Your mum is so going to kill you!

Nah! No problem! Watch this – I'll just turn on the old Ollie charm!

WHAAAT

So much For the old Ollie charm!

...and what's more, you're staying in until you learn to stop breaking expensive things!

Yeah, yeah! And what am I supposed to do in here all day? It's boring!

But my virtual reality skate game isn't – I could play with that!

VIRTUAL SK8ER

Soon...

There! That's me all wired up and ready to go!

Man, this virtual reality thing is sweet...

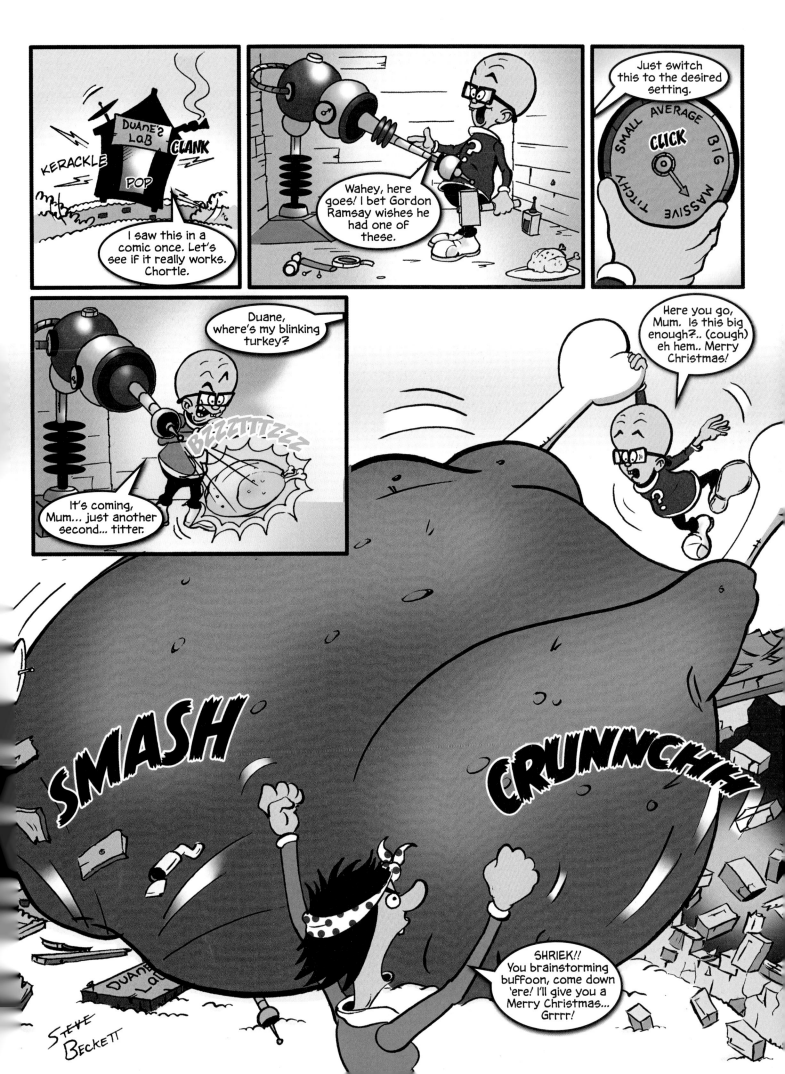

Puss and Boots

Grrrl It's that cheeky cat!

I'm gonna bosh him!

Oof!

CRASH!

RUN

HA! HA! HA! HA! HA! HA! HA! HA!

Boots plans his revenge...

Puss steps on the pressure pad, which trips the anvil...

...then the shark moves in...

...but on E-Bark, the one stop shop for revenge planning dogs, the price of sharks and anvils is way too expensive.

Especially for a dog with no job!

AGENT DOG 2 ZERO

CORPORAL CLOTT

The radar system is a vital part of our nation's defences...

GRAAAA!!!

What is this!?! You, soldier! What are you doing!?!

Er... I'm watching the South East airspace, Colonel Grumbly. In case of an attack on London or Dover!

And...and...I'm watching the North, sir. F-For Russian spy planes!

And what about you, Corporal Clott!?!

I'm watching Ice Age 3. Because... erm, No. I got nothin'.

Come 'ere!!!

Yikes!

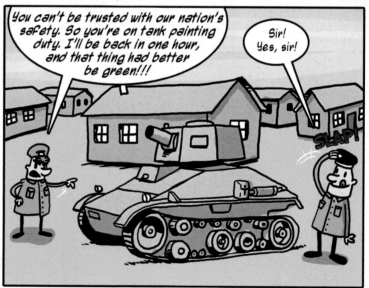

You can't be trusted with our nation's safety. So you're on tank painting duty. I'll be back in one hour, and that thing had better be green!!!

Sir! Yes, sir!

SLAP!

Ow, I hurt my face a bit when I did that salute.

1 hour later...

Corporal Clott's a complete idiot, so what I need to do is stick with jobs like this one. Jobs he can't get wrong.

What!!!

Phew! Just finished in time!

It's pink!!! Why's it pink!?! Pink!!! Why!?!

Something tells me it's not green, is it?

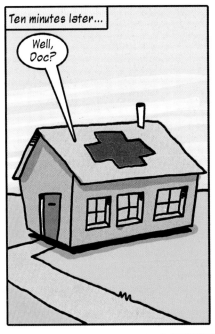

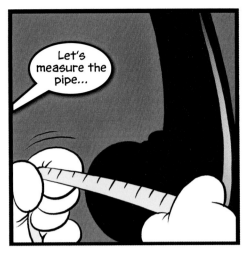

GEORGE vs DRAGON

PRESENTS

"BAYEUX TRAVESTY"

GEORGE WAS A BRAVE AND HANDSOME KNIGHT LOVED BY ALL OF THE LADIES.

ONE DAY GEORGE WAS CALLED UPON BY THE KING OF ENGLAND.

"I NEED YOUR HELP, GOOD KNIGHT" SAID THE KING.

DESPERATE DAN in U.S.A. TOUR PART 3